NOTE TO PARENTS

W9-BSQ-470

Learning to read is an important skill for all children. It is a big milestone that you can help your child reach. The American Museum of Natural History Easy Reader program is designed to support you and your child through this process. Developed by reading specialists, each book in the series includes carefully selected words and sentence structures to help children advance from beginner to intermediate to proficient readers.

Here are some tips to keep in mind as you read these books with your child:

First, preview the book together. Read the title. Then look at the cover. Ask your child, "What is happening on the cover? What do you think this book is about?"

Next, skim through the pages of the book and look at the illustrations. This will help your child use the illustrations to understand the story.

Then encourage your child to read. If he or she stumbles over words, try some of these strategies:

- **use the pictures as clues**
- **point out words that are repeated**
- **sound out difficult words**
- **break up bigger words into smaller chunks**
- **use the context to lend meaning**

Finally, find out if your child understands what he or she is reading. After you have finished reading, ask, "What happened in this book?"

Above all, understand that each child learns to read at a different rate. Make sure to praise your young reader and provide encouragement along the way!

For Heidi Anne, winner of the Roop Seven Continent Contest, who has spent months in Antarctica, home of many penguins. And for Casey, Kelsey, Anna, and Emily. Like Rockhopper Penguins, they will land on their feet as they "rocket" out of college.

—C.R. and P.R.

Photo credits

Cover/title page: © Volodymyr Goinyk/iStockphoto.com
Pages 4–5: © Elenaphotos21/shutterstock; 6–7: © DLILLC/Corbis; 8 (left): © Eric Isselée/shutterstock; 8 (right): © Eric Isselée/shutterstock; 9: © thp73/iStockphoto.com; 10–11: © Jacynth Roode/iStockphoto.com; 10 (inset): © gabor2100/shutterstock; 12: © Tim Davis/Corbis; 13: © Musat Christian/Dreamstime.com; 14–15: © Paulo De Oliveira/Oxford Scientific/Photolibrary; 16–17: © David Hoskins/Photodisc/Getty Images; 18 (left): © GentooMultimediaLimited/iStockphoto.com; 18 (right): © Jordan Tan/shutterstock; 19 (left): © Keith Szafranski/iStockphoto.com; 19 (right): © Linda More/iStockphoto.com; 20: © Auscape/ardea.com; 21: © M. Watson/ardea.com; 22: © John Warburton-Lee Photography/Alamy; 23: Photo courtesy of Phillip Island Nature Parks; 24–25: © H. Reinhard/Arco Images GmbH/Alamy; 26–27: © Roger Tidman/Corbis; 28: © Wolfgang Kaehler/Wolfgang Kaehler Photography; 29 © Photoshot Holdings Ltd./Alamy; 30–31 © kwest/shutterstock; 32 © Evan Sweet

STERLING CHILDREN'S BOOKS
New York

An Imprint of Sterling Publishing
387 Park Avenue South
New York, NY 10016

STERLING CHILDREN'S BOOKS and the distinctive Sterling Children's Books logo are trademarks of Sterling Publishing Co., Inc.

© 2012 by Sterling Publishing Co., Inc., and
The American Museum of Natural History

All rights reserved. No part of this publication may be reproduced, stored in a retrieval system, or transmitted, in any form or by any means, electronic, mechanical, photocopying, recording, or otherwise, without prior written permission from the publisher.

ISBN 978-1-4027-9113-0 (hardcover)
ISBN 978-1-4027-7789-9 (paperback)

Distributed in Canada by Sterling Publishing
c/o Canadian Manda Group, 165 Dufferin Street
Toronto, Ontario, Canada M6K 3H6
Distributed in the United Kingdom by GMC Distribution Services
Castle Place, 166 High Street, Lewes, East Sussex, England BN7 1XU
Distributed in Australia by Capricorn Link (Australia) Pty. Ltd.
P.O. Box 704, Windsor, NSW 2756, Australia

For information about custom editions, special sales, and premium and corporate purchases, please contact Sterling Special Sales at 800-805-5489 or specialsales@sterlingpublishing.com.

Printed in China
Lot #:
2 4 6 8 10 9 7 5 3 1
01/12

www.sterlingpublishing.com/kids

FREE ACTIVITIES & PUZZLES ONLINE AT
http://www.sterlingpublishing.com/kids/sterlingeventkits

PENGUINS ARE COOL!

Connie and Peter Roop

Which bird has flippers and

swims underwater?

A penguin!

Penguins are birds.

They have wings, but they cannot fly.

Penguins use their wings to swim
fast in the water.
They use their feet and tails to turn.

Penguins have two coats of feathers.

Penguins also have a layer of fat
under their skin.

This fat keeps penguins warm.

Some penguins live in very cold places,

like on this ice.

But some penguins live in warmer

places, too.

This map shows all the places where penguins nest.

Penguins swim in Earth's
southern oceans.
They swim in cold water even if
they live in warmer places.

A penguin's colors help it hide from enemies.
Penguins have dark backs that look like the dark water below them.

Penguins have white bellies that look like light from the sun above.

A penguin's colors keep it safe from predators above and below.

Penguins spend most of their time
in the ocean.
They even eat there.

This Gentoo Penguin is about to catch a fish.
It catches food with its beak and holds on to it.

Penguins spend most of their time
in the water.
But they lay their eggs on land.

These Gentoo Penguins build nests.

They sit on their eggs to keep

them warm.

Many kinds of penguins swim in Earth's southern oceans.

Emperor Penguins are the tallest penguins.
Little Blue Penguins are the smallest penguins.

Macaroni Penguins and Rockhopper Penguins have colorful feathers on their heads.

The mother Emperor Penguin

lays an egg.

The father Emperor Penguin puts

the egg on his feet to keep it warm.

The chick is born!

The chick stands on its father's feet.

The father penguin keeps the

chick warm.

Little Blue Penguins live in Australia
and New Zealand.
They lay their eggs in holes.

The chicks are fluffy and brown.
When the chicks are about two months old, they lose their brown feathers and grow blue and white ones.

Macaroni Penguins dance.

Then the females lay their eggs.

They wave their bright yellow
head feathers as they dance.

Rockhopper Penguins jump out of the water onto rocks to lay their eggs. Rockhopper Penguins can hop five feet to reach a rock!

How high can you hop?

Some penguins slide on their bellies. They move like sleds across the snow and ice.

Sometimes penguins slide down an icy hill on their big feet.
This is another way penguins can move fast.

Penguins can be tall or small.

They slip and slide.

Penguins swim, walk, eat, and nest.

Penguins are cool birds!

MEET THE EXPERT!

My name is **Paul Sweet**, and I am an ornithologist—a scientist who studies birds. I have been interested in birds since I was a young boy growing up in the English countryside. So, being able to work with birds is a childhood dream come true! I now work at the American Museum of Natural History. There, I manage a vast collection of almost one million bird specimens that has been assembled over two centuries by explorers, scientists, and even presidents.

In addition to working with this amazing collection at the Museum, I travel all over the world to study birds in places like the Solomon Islands and the mountains of Vietnam, where there are still many things to discover about the birds that live there. This work helps us understand why birds live in different places and how they interact with their habitats. In addition, studying birds can help protect their habitats. I help gather information so that conservation groups can save the birds that live in that area.

Penguins have always fascinated me because they are so different from other birds. I think one of the most remarkable things about them is the different ways they have adapted to their varied environments—from the equator to the Antarctic. Working with birds like these is really amazing—I love being an ornithologist!